CW00418938

You're Not Alone

Pain's Great Wisdom

Also Available on eBook and Paperback

A Shenanigans Tale: Soot, Whisky and Ho Ho's
A Shenanigans Tale: War, Tape and Tinsel

You're Not
Alone
Pain's Great Wisdom

A Collection of Words and Poetry
by K. J. Broadhurst

Copyright © 2019 K.J. Broadhurst

First published in Great Britain in 2019
By K.J. Broadhurst
The Right of K.J. Broadhurst to be identified as the author of the work has been asserted by him in
accordance with the Copyright, Design and Patents Act 1988

1

All rights reserved. Apart from any use permitted under UK copyright law, this publication may not
be reproduced, stored or transmitted, in any form, or by any means without prior permission in
writing from the publishers and may not be otherwise circulated in any form of binding or cover
other than that which it is published and without a similar condition being imposed on the
subsequent purchaser.
All characters in this publication are fictitious and any resemblance to real persons, living or dead
is purely coincidental.
A Catalogue record for this book is available from the British Library

ISBN 978 1087260303
www.kjbroadhurst.com

For Amelia and Ruby
One lost and One Dreamt

Index

Foreword

Life has moments of joy and moments of anguish. It is during the latter that anyone can feel the most alone, without someone to turn to or holding the belief that no one else can understand or appreciate what suffering is.

Within the following works, the bleakest moments of human nature are explored and considered – K. J. Broadhurst himself has suffered but has put his feelings into writing, showing that no one is alone when feeling depressed, or that the world is on top of them, and the feelings of pain are as natural as going to sleep or having a drink.

Easing this pain is not easy, as shown by the following poems, and can sometimes lead to the most drastic consideration of all. But someone will always be there, someone will always listen as long as you know where to look. And in terms of suffering you're not alone.

Nick Bartlett
Editor and Friend

Introduction by the Author

As a way of managing how I feel I express this through words. Talking has never come easily to me and my writing, in the past has gotten me in a lot of trouble, especially as a child. What is interesting is I am seeing the same in my children, particularly my middle son Conner, who has developed a flair for writing himself.

I am a writer. I don't claim to be a great one, nor do I expect to be the next great thing, but I love to write and that makes me a writer, and if you are the same that makes you a writer too. As a writer what makes us different, is that we write not just for ourselves (though much of it is) but we can't be writers if our words, thoughts and feelings are not read. They don't have to be liked or appreciated, though that is nice from time to time, but it's a writer's way to make themselves heard. That may be through fiction or it may be fact - indeed most fiction is still built on some level of truth that's what makes the best liars. This book of poems is my truth.

It is simply that, my truth.

As a writer who likes to have any excuse to write, I could go into great detail about each poem, tell you the story behind it, but that's my story, and though I am sharing the poems, these are not stories but more moments. Moments of fear, sadness, confusion, loss and happiness. Some are happy (all be it not many) but if I was happy all the time, I would have nothing to write about - like the famous Adele who has openly admitted she can only write when she's miserable. By not telling you about each poem this allows you to connect with it, what resonates in you and why. That is personal to you, and if you connect with that poem, if it stirs emotions in you, then it is yours, I give it to you. I appreciate these are very personal to me, but I actually feel this book is very much aimed for the men *out there who are struggling with their emotions. Despite some of our greatest poets being men (my favourite being Simon Armitage) I don't feel many men really set out to read poetry. Yet men deal with sadness, heartbreak, loss and so many other emotions very differently than women and that is what has also prompted me to publish this. Men do feel, we get depressed, upset but how we express this is different, maybe it's traditional, cultural or even genetic? But I want to share with you my 'moments' and maybe you too can find your way to express yourself rather than suffer on your own.*

In writing and publishing this, I have sinned having unleashed this wallowie book of free style that is the ultimate hate of any 'real poet'. Prior to the publication I asked a handful of therapists and friends, who all have experience in working with the emotions that I am writing about in this book, to ask their opinions and thoughts. The response was mixed but the one comment, that hit home the most was how the poems were personal but wallowie. I have taken that on board and thought hard about whether I should go ahead and publish this after all. You can tell what my decision was so, why still publish? Well, firstly the Heather (Bach Flower Remedies) in me could not resist and second there seems to be a genuine interest in my work. In the future I know I'll look back and cringe, but it is how I feel now (or then as the case may be) and because I believe in my work and my voice.

This book is very much based on my experience of love. I have been lucky enough to find true love, but also unlucky enough to lose it. Still, I hold on in hope, though it feels an impossibility but without hope we have little else to look forward to. Failing that we have the memories and move forward to build new ones based upon a clean foundation.

Life is a layer of cement; once a layer of brick is in place, we can then add another but it's never too late to change the colour!

One last thing. Ballads and songs about love and break up - listen to the ones written and sung by men and written and sung by woman. Notice the difference? I'll leave that with you. I hope you enjoy this book and if you ever wish to contact me, feel free just visit the website.

Love and Light
K.J. Broadhurst
www.kjbroadhurst.com

An Unlikely Proposal

The day is bright
when you are near
your smile,
your laugh makes all become clear
I can't imagine a
day without you
so I have no choice but
to ask, if I can marry you?

I know the timing
is not well planned
I know the future
appears unclear and mad
but all I ask is
for you to look into
my eyes and see,
will you my love,
will you marry me?

Be True

When you feel worthless, sad and alone no one cares to see... but when you stand tall, say I'm worth more and deserve to be heard everyone suddenly stops and takes notice. They will cast judgment on you and choose a side and the world you know is no more. Yet your past is like your shadow, it is always there behind you, following you wherever you go, but as long as you keep walking towards the light the shadow that is your past will never consume you.

Bursting Passion

All around me are stories of love
of passionate nights
and romancing under starry sights
I hear of their wild adventures
knees carpet deep
among glistening candle lights
I want your nails to cut so deep
to hold me so close
that no light should seep
I need your warm breast
and your tender thighs
to cradle me with warm surprise
I crave to kiss you on the neck
not stopping until I reach
the soul of your step
I dream of feeling
your hands clench tight
at our mattress every single night
I want to hear my name echo the walls
to break behind your female walls
to hear you gasp against sweaty pores
but rather I wake to your deep snores
the frustration scrambling with my head
waiting for the passion I am so eager to shed

Cords

True love did not exist until the day I met you,
those owl-like eyes, the curls, the depth of the brown
the smile and the pull I felt on my
eternal cords, telling me I belong to you

The feeling was mutual, circumstances not
I had the strength and you did not
we were happy together, hand in hand, arm in arm,
yet my empty pockets were not what you needed

We both had ties, we both had heartbreak
we both wanted one thing, but that thing became
to easy to break
with lies, need, lust it was a mistake

We forgot the cords that drew us together
our destinies fulfilled
yet you opted for the easy life,
the house, the cat and not a wife

Now empty and alone I watch your material
happiness, bitterness and regret,
I was your mistake, the cords are broken
shattered, severing what kept me whole

Heartbroken

Cruel Power

No male holds power to condemn
like you and your female honour betrayed
torn between guilt and love
Yet a message of all is well from above
discussions forced and then made
could our blessed be also afraid
as IT is human
The watery depths of my emotions a metaphor
the fires of our wills, clash
what of the love that we made?
Oh how no other being can achieve what you will
call it innocence, call it surrender
once done, it is done forever

The Final Dilemma

Does the sun continue to rise?
As I shut my eyes for the last time

Can I hear the crashing waves?
As I take my final breath

Will I meet with loved ones once more?
Holding close those I adore

Can I still watch my family grow?
Help them through with my gentle glow

Can I still hold them to my breast?
Guiding them though as I know best

Stop their pain with a wave of my hand?
As they struggle across the weighing sand

It cannot be the final setting of the moon?
Leaving nothing but darkness

Sadness, tears and gloom
This must be another page of life's lies

But surely nobody ever really dies?

Guides

Tom makes his way to work as usual, the night silent and cool. In the corner of his
eye he glimpses a stray's eyes, following him meaningfully. The stray wonders whether
this man knows what is coming, his mind lost. The stray leaves, for another will
wait. Tom feels unnerved by the strange activity of these stray creatures, standing
like soldiers at their allocated posts. There is suddenly a bright light behind, it's shadow creeping,
there is a cry. Tom feels light as he is no longer on his feet. He sees his little boy, warm in
his cot and his sweetheart, before all around is hold and standing over him are two bulging
eyes reflective and warm. Before they explode with light.

I am Sorry

I have so much to apologise for,
My temper
My impatience
But I do not apologise for my
vengeance

There is only so many times
You can say no
And I'm not the priority
But I love you so much
I hold on, I am sorry

Your beauty and your heart are
Astonishing to me
so are the lies
That you relayed daily to me
But I am sorry

I can forgive all the lies you shared
The hurt
The pain
To just have a chance to hold you again
For that I am sorry

What I did was right and just,
You wanted cake
You wanted lust
You wanted to be loved, have a home
For that I am sorry

I cannot give you what you have yet
The house
The pets
love I can give, unconditional
And true, I am sorry

If you can forgive me,
Draw a line
Start again
Put me first in your life, I won't
Ever have to be sorry again

But I am sorry

Let's try again

Three is not enough you know,
I want to try again,
a boy a girl or even twins
How about it then?
Take *em* off
or pull *em* to one side
it's gonna be quite a ride
Brace yourself and count to ten,
have a breath and start again

Not over but complete

Love is a book with chapters,
You move on with the page, even
Though you keep reading on,
You can go back and re-read what
Is done
And when you close the pages
And the story is but over
You can go back and read the bits
You loved,
The story is never over

Persist

He
Is unwise to expect
Success
Disappointment
For little or nothing
Occurs

Good failures
Are
As helpful
And as educated
As
Grand success

He
Is thoughtful
Observant
And endeavours to ascertain
The cause
Of no success

He
Will realise
Stimulated
Activity
As influences
Are at work

Only patience
And experience

Will
Permit him
To be
Open and responsive

He
In the meantime
Must
Just do
His
Best

The Dark

I look into your eyes, etched into my memory
As I take the last pill
A swig of spirit, drowning in my own tears
I settle for the dark
The swirl of our memories, the laughter
I allow myself to smile
Pain is building, the burning deadly
Yet it is nothing
I can feel my shell going numb, prickling
Soon I will be gone
The last image I see is you not with me, happy
And I allow myself to be taken

Unknown

Even though our time was short
Your presence hardly known

I looked at you, where you lay
In your mother's womb

Just her skin and your safe walls
Were all I had to see

But Just for that one moment
I kissed you passionately

At the time it was the first
And never did I see

That the walls keeping you safe
Would be invaded so brutally

There you lay so cold and bare
No love just pain, with that I share

The tears the fears and all alone
My beautiful baby

Unknown

Voice of Druids

His heart is torn by the waves of emotion
But his strength is a rock of passion and devotion
Despite the shelter of that dark black cloud
If he speaks with the voice from his heart
And allows the tears to fall freely, proud
Will open him up to those long since gone
His psychic powers sharp and strong
Wings will then open to the echoes of the gentle breeze
He will hear its warm sound as nature sings
And shall rise above the tearing waves,
With grace and with wisdom, a natural leader
Watching down upon God's kingdom

Love is no Fairy Tale

True love is no fairy tale it doesn't come with ease
It can strike at any time, and inappropriately it seems,

It's timing a deadly landmine, we will dodge every bomb
Hands snug, fitting perfectly as if made for one

Treading every piece of stone and every grain of sand,
we watch the sun rise and we watch each step land.

Time is fast, yet time is borrowed we press on with hope and
trepidation down this uncertain road

A sudden mishap, who was to blame? We are swiftly blown apart;
one was thrown, and one was smart

We are battered we are bruised, we attempt to recover, yet it is
long, one on their own and one with another

Life without each other, is the worst pain to bare, no bed, no
medicine can we share. Are hands no longer fit,

no glue, no splint can mould them back together. Too Distorted by
grief and broken deep, hearts closed, no happy ever after

We watched the sun rise and we watched the sun set, let's not
forget, time was love time was true and it was no lie when I said I
love you

Love is not a fairy tale the time was just
not right, we used each other to see the stars and when we did

the stars were bright

Life is Hell

The feeling of heavy lead
The gurgling, the sickness
The butterflies, elation
How can anyone create
Such tension
Going to burst, going to cry
Going to cut myself
Or at least try
Nothing - no blade, no pill
Can heal yet there is no will
The feeling reminds me that I am
Alive but I want to be dead
No light at the end, no one
To hold, no one to tell,
No one to offer my soul,
Not even to sell
It is eroding,
it is poisoned, diseased,
your cold logic
Condemning me.
There is no air
To breathe, I am breathless
My life is over, it is relentless

Words that Lie

Is there no happiness,
No positive word to express.
I try so hard to bring that
Ghastly word to transgress,
happiness!
What is it
I found it
I lost it
Happiness that putrid emotion
To fool us into selfless
Devotion

My Green Eyes

This once beating organ,
Is bleeding through my chest
Leaving no comfort, no rest
Time together had mended
And made me whole
Just artificial now poisoning my soul
Cradling the blanket
That kept you warm, the sweet
Drug that I have to inhale
Knowing it won't last
Like us its sweetness was comfort
But now it's just pain. The
Poison so deep I don't feel I can
Remain sane. Like a virus unavoidable
Now the temperature soughs
Nothing can ease it, no potions, no cures
Can I survive this, no antidotes
except yours

The Funny Side?

As kids' life was fun, just a daily routine and mothers nagging, now at thirty it's about money and checking my bums not sagging Work is mundane, boring and long made no simpler since the kids come along. No promotion, no raise just getting by and accumulating the debts knowing my wife has been buying buy one get one frees and pointless box sets.

As I leave off work I know as soon as I walk in, the kids will be crawling the ceiling, the wife screaming at them to no avail and the dog will be fighting off the baby as he swings from its tail Once they have been yanked, gathered up, pulled away it's time for supper and then bed, having to read the same old bloody story wishing you were dead.

The only thing left in life to look forward to was THE bath in the hope the wife was feeling frisky, instead the only pleasure is a can of coke and a bottle of whisky.

Sex is like a swear word, say it you'll get stung, and you watch as she changes to get a glimpse of her peachy bum.

Oh, don't look, you perv, I hate myself, I feel fat I feel worthless, so instead we go without me lying in a cold bed in boxers and shirtless. And they wonder why when some other beauty comes along, you look knowing it's wrong but when they say your wonderful, you're handsome you're reminded of the screaming, that same old story, the declaration that you're a perv because of what the wife was revealing.

Feeling lonely, feeling worthless, you look and dare to wonder what else this shit life might have to offer, and you allow it to happen, you dare to dream only to be the arsehole who wandered off with a beauty, who offers sex, love and endless opportunity

The Station Girl

From the Unpublished Button Holes
2007

The Station Girl

Annie Tomas watched in bewilderment as the trees firmly rooted in the ground and the sheep that stood grazing in the fields raced by. The tip of her nose was pressed against the glass of the carriage window, its surface ice-cold upon her warm skin. She giggled to herself and her excited breath formed condensation, which her small hands wiped away as she tried to stay focused on the trees and sheep as they rushed past. No matter how hard she tried, the trees and sheep would always outrun her.

She was a pretty little girl, with bright blonde hair and a sweet round face; small freckles dotted round her rosy cheeks and nose.

Suddenly the train juddered.

Annie jerked sideways, forcing her against her mother, dropping one of her two teddy bears. Annie went to lean forward, attempting to reach for Brownie, when something tugged hard, forcing her back to an up-right position. Annie gasped as her pink t-shirt cut into her throat. Dazed, she looked up at her mother, her joyful expression gone and her eyes glazed with tears.

Annie's mother gazed down upon her daughter, face fierce. Her wide eyes were dark brown daggers staring at her prey without an ounce of love in her expression.

She did not speak, just glared, abusing her power over Annie, which was intoxicating.

Annie looked away, head down, ashamed of what she had done. She was a bad girl and she knew it. In her anguish, she embraced her second teddy. She cuddled it so close that if he were alive, she would surely suffocate him, squeezing so tight, desperate to find comfort in his grubby blue fur. Annie loved her teddies. They were her friends. They never looked at her like her mother did. They didn't shout at her or hurt her. They were always there, ready for a hug or a chat. They loved her and she loved them.

The journey was long. Annie sat frozen, her arms tightly wrapped around her blue bear, despairing as Brownie lay rocking side to side with the jerking and shuddering of the train. A tear trickled down her now pale cheek as she watched her poor bear, her poor friend, helpless on the dirty floor. Annie was growing more and more desperate to get to him, to hold and tell him he was safe. She was his mummy who was supposed to look after and protect him. But she was too scared to reach forward to save him. That was bad. That was wrong and her mother would be angry if she did that. Despairing, she thought, *it must be cold down there*. She watched on helpless at her companion lying on the floor, all alone. Her tummy ached with the tension of fear and loneliness. Then Annie had an idea.

She turned to her small pink bag that sat comfortably beside her. Unbuttoning it, she pulled out a screwed up and worn Thomas the tank engine pillowcase. She called it Ticky. She would wrap her teddies up in it at night, to keep them warm, just in case her duvet slid off as she turned in her sleep. Annie pulled it out; carefully trying to aim it so that it would fall comfortably over Brownie's body, but to her horror the pillowcase covered his whole face.

Annie slammed forward.

Her mother's hand was held high over her daughter's head.

Annie did not shout or scream - neither did she raise her hands protectively, she just held her blue teddy tightly.

"What are you doing, you stupid little girl?" Her mother bellowed.

Annie stayed where she was frozen, hunched over her teddy, hardly daring to move, worried that her mother would hit her again. Tears began to bleed from her beautiful green eyes, trickling down her soft skin, falling from her chin and absorbing into Blue Bear's fur.

The train came to a halt and crowds of people were soon on their feet, cramming to get off the train, pushing and shoving. Annie's mother stood up, her frame large and frightening.

Apprehensively Annie hopped off the seat, finally picking up her bear. She had been right. Brownie was very cold. She embraced him lovingly, "I'm sorry Brownie, I won't ever drop you again," she whispered, her voice motherly.

She moved to leave the train, struggling to keep up with her mother, who was marching ahead. Annie's bag was hanging off her left arm as she held her teddy's hands. Their small bodies dangling suspended from the ground. Still behind her mother, who was stepping down onto the platform, Annie noticed Ticky was falling out of the bag. She paused to tuck him back in, when she was knocked forward, losing her balance, stumbling onto all fours. She dropped both her bears; although she had managed to tuck Ticky safely back into the bag before stumbling. She went to pick up Blue Bear, but realised that Brownie was missing, again. She looked round desperately to find him, to hold him close, but he was not there. Where was he?

"Brownie, Brownie," she shouted, crying out for her bear, "Brownie, where are you?" but the bear did not appear or answer her.

She saw her mother storming towards her. Trepidation pumping through every vein, Annie bravely looked up at her mother's bulging face and cried: "Mummy, Brownie! I can't find him, I can't find Brownie!"

Her mother looked down at her, furious and bitter. To Annie she looked like a big round monster with curly hair.

"Get up!" her mother demanded, grabbing her daughter, hauling Annie to her feet.

"Mummy! Brownie!" Annie cried urgently for her mother to help in the search.

"Shut up about your stupid bear!" her mother hissed blushing in embarrassment, seizing Annie again.

"No Brownie! I want Brownie!" Annie choked.

"Will you be quiet?"

Still Annie persisted.

"Shut up! You stupid little girl! It's only a bear! Do you know how silly you look? Everyone is looking at you. What do you think they are saying, ha?" Her mother's face inches away from her daughters. "You're embarrassing me," She hissed through clenched teeth.

Annie's head was down, sobbing uncontrollably, wanting her Brownie, wanting her mother to help her.

"Everyone is looking at you", her voice was nothing but a whisper. "They're saying look at that silly little girl."

Annie was not really listening, focusing on the floor of the train, still scanning, frantically, trying to find her lost teddy.

Her mother, who still had a tight grip of her pink top, hauled her forward off the train, Annie's head still down. And as she was dragged off the train and onto the platform: *there he was*. Brownie was laying on the track itself, deep between the train and the platform – looking up at her. *It's dark down there*, she thought, only just being able to see his small shape.

"Mummy, mummy, down there," she sobbed and pointed, but her mother continued to shepherd her forward. Annie pulled back. She had to save Brownie; her little teddy from the dark.

"Mummy, no Brownie, Brownie!" she screamed, "Brownie doesn't like the dark mummy, mummy please mummy, no please, help me get Brownie, please mummy please!"

But her mother just tugged her away from her bear, from the dark where he lay getting cold. And as Annie was marched out of the station, she took one last desperate look back before she began to sob, mourning the loss of her friend Brownie, who she promised she would never drop again. She had failed him just like she had always disappointed her mother whom she loved. So, she just stared at the floor, silent, as they exited the station.

A Shenanigans Tale
Soot, Whisky and Ho Ho's
2012

Soot, Whisky and Ho Ho's

The bittersweet glow of lamplight exhibited a feeling of warmth and serenity in the room. Patrick stood at the extinguished fireplace and took from the oak surround a glass of whisky, which he swirled in an anti-clockwise motion, the amber liquid sloshing thickly. He made his way over to his armchair, which he had inherited from his great-grandfather when he was twenty-two and slumped himself down contently before taking a sip of his recently acquired beverage. Patrick allowed, with great pleasure, the liquid to slide smoothly down his throat, feeling its delightfully warm trail run all the way down into his stomach: bliss. His wife Annie was out with friends and his two boys James and William were in bed fast asleep. He had enjoyed spending the evening with them both without Annie there to nag him. They had baked fresh chocolate cookies from scratch-something he had not done since high school - and allowed the two boys to pour four fingers of his best whisky to put out for Santa, which he now held; the glass fitting snugly in his grasp, as if made especially for the occasion. Annie would not be home until past midnight, so she had left Patrick to arrange and pack the presents into the children's individual Santa sacks, ready for the morning. This was something he was determined to leave right to the last minute, savouring this precious time to sit back and relax, allowing his mind to wonder without the constant 'dad, dad!' and 'am I left to do everything round here!' With that thought, he took another sip.

All of a sudden, there was a strange bang from above. Patrick, with the glass at his lips, sat motionless, his ears erect and listening tentatively. There it was again, a thudding noise like footsteps. They had experienced problems before with mice and rats, which was something one excepted when living in the country and next to a spring. But this sounded different, heavier somehow.

There was a scraping sound and then abruptly soot rained down from the chimney. Patrick froze. Two eyes appeared, looking straight at him upside down from under the mantelpiece. The whites of his eyes were more obvious than the whiteness of his hair, which hung down thinly like silver tinsel. Instinctively Patrick put his glass in his left hand, freeing up the other to grasp hold of the small antique coffee table, which stood beside him. 'Wha...wha...what are you doing in my house?' Patrick uttered, attempting to sound threatening but unable to hide the shaking in his voice. The intruder clumsily came to his feet with an explosion of soot and then ducked as he stepped out of the fireplace. He brushed himself off and smiled, 'Hello me old son.' Patrick's face was a picture of shock and horror. Not only had he got an intruder in his house, but the imposter had now made a ghastly mess of his prized cream carpet. No one was allowed in this room, except in the evenings to watch television and to relax. They most definitely did not tolerate under any circumstances... shoes. This was a slipper or bare foot only zone. Yet at this precise moment, two large boots, blackened with chimney soot, now stood before him. Once he was able to deter his mortified eyes from the soot-smothered boots, he noticed a short dumpy man dressed in a red sports tracksuit. He had a mousey face, short-cut white beard and thin, silvery hair. 'That by the way,' said the intruder pointing at his whisky glass, 'was put out for me, so if you don't mind, I'll go get myself another?' Without consent the intruder made his way over to the drink's cabinet, which stood in the corner of the room and pored himself a generous measure of Patrick's finest whisky liqueur. He then took a long sip and sat his sooty backside on the caramel couch, the bottle still in hand. Patrick stood grasping the coffee table. 'Who the hell are you? What gives you the right too...'

'You know who I am; otherwise you would've chucked that thing at me by now.' Patrick glanced at the weapon, as if surprised it was even there and then put it down. 'I must be going mad, you don't exist,' he whispered.

'Said like a true skeptic and like all true skeptic's you're just too frightened to believe.'

'I am not frightened!'

The intruder snorted in a jolly manner, 'you could have fooled me.'

'It's not possible for you to exist. How can you travel all over the world in one-night hum?'

The man laughed again whole heartedly. 'And like a true skeptic you have to see it to believe it.' Patrick sat himself back down again. 'Why don't I tell you who I am and then explain how I do, in fact, exist?' Patrick, unable to speak, just nodded foolishly. 'Here,' said the intruder, 'have some more of this, it will help,' and he leaned over the arm of the couch and topped up Patricks glass. 'Now,' he said before leaning back, 'I do exist: I have nine incredible reindeer, of which Dancer and Prancer have been an item for over one hundred years now; Blitzen is my chief inventor, and like me they can all speak every language. The only thing that is seriously wrong with your stories are, I don't go around delivering presents in one night to every good child, now that would truly be impossible, and I don't live with a community of elves either.'

'So, what's the point?' said Patrick, 'If you don't deliver presents then why do you exist and why for that matter are you here drinking my whisky?' Santa smiled, 'That's the best bit' he said, 'I have my reindeer because I do deliver the odd present to those who are most worthy of it, but the rest is done telepathically.'

That was it.

'What are you, some kind of nut job escaped from the nearest prison? Did you really believe I would fall for this crap? GET OUT!' Patrick was on his feet again, coffee table in hand. Santa however, did not budge, or even look the slightest bit frightened. Instead, he just smiled again, more widely and cheerfully than before. 'How was it then, that when you were walking home from work the day before yesterday that all of a sudden you had a thought? In that split second you knew, as if out of thin air, what to get your little boy William for Christmas.' Slightly taken aback by the statement, Patrick lowered the coffee table, perplexed. How on earth could he have known that? Santa pointed his small sausage-like finger at him and laughed. 'Got you there didn't I?' he said draining the last of his whisky, then filling it up again. 'But how...?'

'Sit down old chap and I will explain.'

Patrick did as he asked. Without thinking, he drained all of his whiskey in one go.

'Your stories tell children that Santa and his helpers work all year round, making the presents that will, if good, end up in their stockings. That I'm afraid doesn't work and cannot work. Imagine what China would have to say about that?' he laughed, 'No. I spend the year asleep. I sit on a very comfortable chair and tune myself into what you may call a psychic network. Once I am connected, I can hear the thoughts of all the children in the world. I can hear their pleas, their wishes and their dreams and, I do all that I can to help them. I don't just give presents. I also help them find the support they need. In this trance like state, I can focus on one thought and manipulate it, or add a completely new thought, like yours the other day. Therefore, you could say Santa does bring the boys and girls their presents because I provide the ideas that encourages you - the parent - to buy them.'

'So, you can get into other people's heads and put things in there.'

'If that's how you see it, then yes, that is exactly what I do.'

'And drink other people's whisky,' Patrick offered sarcastically.

'Why not hey?' he laughed again. 'You do have good stuff here, so good in fact, I'll just have to have another.' It was in this moment Patrick realised that he himself had had quite a lot to drink and was beginning to feel the effects. Was that why he was accepting this stranger and his mad explanations? His head was beginning to swim, but this man seemed pleasant enough, even if he was completely insane!

'What you haven't said,' began Patrick, 'is why you lumbered down my chimney, got soot all over my expensive carpet and why you are on my couch drinking my favourite whisky?'

'Ho ho,' Santa jeered. 'That is a good question. The reason I am here is because you asked me to be here,' said the jolly man, now adding even more whisky to his glass. In his bewilderment, Patrick noticed that the bottle was now nearly empty. Had they really drunk nearly a whole bottle of the stuff... and neat?

'I never asked for you to come here?' Patrick objected.

'So, you never sat in your chair and wished your partner would go out for just one evening and, that your two boys would sleep early so that you could have a relaxing evening without nagging or children crying?'

'Well I...'

'Have you not... sat and wished you had someone to talk too and drink whisky with? Because when you do go out, you either have to drive, or drive someone?'

'Well yes but...'

'And here I am. I ensured that all thoughts were cleared from both your boys' heads and put the suggestions in the right minds to get you partner to go out for the evening, two birds with one stone and all that.' Dumbfounded Patrick could say nothing at all. 'I have also brought you a gift. Your hard work over the last year hasn't gone unnoticed, well by me anyway,' Santa said, and he began to rummage inside his jacket. 'Ah, here it is!' he declared. Santa Claus made his way across the room to the television, where he painfully knelt to put a DVD into the player. 'It's HD so should look quite something on your 51-inch TV.'

'What is it?' asked Patrick.

'Let's just say - for all your hard work - you'll be the first person to see this and I am sure you will thank me for it.' The screen came to life and there in front of him was the main menu for the Doctor Who Christmas Special.

'I don't...How?'

'Have you not been listening to what I have been telling you? Not only have I just sat and told the truth about me but also what I can do.' 'I know but how did you get hold of this?'

'Easy, I just made a very nasty and greedy man who works within the BBC make a copy of this disc and walk away with it, before making him feel guilty where he then chucked it into the bin, where I then just happened to pass and pick it up.'

A smile wider than any smile he had offered in nearly four years spread over Patrick's face. 'Am I dreaming or is this really the Christmas Special?'

'Press play and see,' said Santa, grinning merrily in response to Patrick's delight. 'Like I said before, your hard work this year has not gone unnoticed.' Patrick did so and there, right before his eyes, the DVD began and soon he was watching his favourite television programme a whole twenty-four hours before it would be broadcast to the rest of the country. He did not speak or look anywhere else other than the television screen through the whole episode. When it was finished, he went to turn and say thank you to this magical man, but he was not there. The couch was empty and next to it on the coffee table was a fresh bottle of whisky with a red ribbon round it. He stood and held the bottle before him, reading the tag, which hung from the ribbon:

Don't forget to wrap the presents, or you'll be in for it! I've laid out two brand new sacks, which I think both your boys will appreciate and I have tidied up.

Love and best wishes Santa

P.S. You'll need to watch your boy James and make sure he looks out for an old woman named Aggie!

With that, Patrick wrapped all the presents, and once he was done, he sat back and watched the DVD again: bliss

Acknowledgments

I would like to take this opportunity to thank Nathalie, my childhood sweetheart, friend and partner for the past 17 years. We have come full circle but have remained friends. Everything that could be said has been said but I still am sorry for the way it ended. We had amazing times and I will hold on to those and we will still work as a team to bring up our three amazing children. I wish you all the happiness and if you ever need a friend I'll never be far away, and I love you.

A huge thank you to be best and dearest friend Nick. You have been there in my darkest times; you have never judged, and you have stood by me when so many would not have done and whom subsequently haven't. I hope that one day I can be the friend to you that you have been to me, and to your mum who let's be honest, has been the voice a reason.

So many people today look up to their heroes who are footballers, actors and celebrities, but Tessa you are mine. You do something none of these heroes do and that is not to press your own views on us, instead you nurture and guide us to be the best we can be following our own truths. You really are special, and your every word has a value to me, and I always listen. I thank you for being you and being there since I was just a little boy. Yes, it was your job, but you have always taken care of me, putting my health and wellbeing before your own benefit. There are just not the words to express how thankful I am to you.

Also my Circle Ruth, Kate, Andre, Melody, Caz, Caron, Patsy and Donner to name a few you have been a great support and it's been such a pleasure working with you all, Jo who has de-knotted and offered the words needed at that time and continues to do so. To all my family, my grandmother, to my sister in-law Sophie, who offered a hug on New Year's when I was secretly falling apart, I will never forget that, and of course to my boys who keep me inspired and moving forward. There have been many times that I have considered giving up but you three pull me out every time.

Green Eyes, despite everything I forgive you. I have nothing to apologize for. I loved you, I have never denied it to myself or to anyone else.

I have so many amazing Leo's in my life that I must thank, Nathalie, Nick, Granny, Stefan, Jo, but one other deserves a mention too, Judith you brought a little class back into my life, supported me and made the days a little more beautiful. Hold on in there we need you!

Thank you to all of you and all the others I have not mentioned here.

K.J. Broadhurst

Coming Soon

The Shenanigans of Aggies Elbow
September 2020

28386088R00035

Printed in Great Britain
by Amazon